on down the road

on down the road

**Haiku Society of America
2017 Members' Anthology**

**LeRoy Gorman
Editor**

**Haiku Society of America
New York**

on down the road

ISBN: 978-1-930172-17-3

Each poem in this anthology was chosen by the editor from a selection of published and unpublished haiku and senryu submitted by current members of the Haiku Society of America. Each participating member has one poem in the anthology.

Cover photo and cover design: Luminita Suse

Book production: Mike Montreuil

Book layout: Lynda Wegner — www.freshimage.ca

Introduction

The title of this year's anthology and its contents are a homage to Basho and his seminal work *Oku no Hosomichi (Narrow Road to the Far North)*. For many of the poets here, Basho's writing first inspired them to become travelers and embark on the haiku road.

On this road, there are travelers who have long been on the journey alongside recent arrivals. And, as one might expect, the vehicles they operate come in different shapes and sizes. These include everything from seventeen syllable poems written in a 5/7/5 format to compact models of only a few syllables. Three-line poems are most common but a number appear anywhere from one to as many as nine lines. The themes, as well, are no less various. There are poems about nature, city life, death and taxes, love and lust, freedom and imprisonment, war and peace, time and space, and more.

Behind all the variance, there is a striking commonality— the sense that all poets put forth work that captures a significant poetic moment they can be proud of. Kath Abela Wilson, for one, states, "When I wrote this I was so happy to have been able to capture a very strong childhood experience— I still have chills when I think of it, on the ferries from Staten Island and Brooklyn . . . I had tried before, but this time it really felt like the real thing." This idea of achieving *the real thing* occurs over and over in the work of 351 contributors who have come from around the globe to travel Basho's road.

Once the on ramp is taken, the reader is will find that what was once a narrow road is now a bustling highway that shows no signs of quieting.

LeRoy Gorman
Editor

on down the road

the sound of snap peas
picked and dropped into her pail
summer rain

Meredith Ackroyd
Afton, Virginia

prettier
this year than last . . .
perennials

Dennise Aiello
Benton, Louisiana

little fly
too swift to trap
mi casa tu casa

Fred Andrle
Columbus, Ohio

he threatens
to sell again
the crunch of a snail's shell

Bett Angel-Stawarz
Barmera, South Australia, Australia

that winter whiskey bottle after whiskey bottle

frances angela
London, England

new moon
I regret asking
how he voted

Susan Antolin
Walnut Creek, California

first rainbow
the start-ups' founders
are all immigrants

Fay Aoyagi
San Francisco, California

morning mist
mountains climb slowly
into new day

Jim Applegate
Roswell, New Mexico

cold clouds
subway seats full
of cell phones

Eric Arthen
Worthington, Massachusetts

picking apples
the expectations
I can't reach

Marilyn Ashbaugh
Edwardsburg, Michigan

dusk
bush warbler's song shapes it—
peace

Francis Attard
Marsa, Malta

flickering flame
the woman behind me
sings the high notes

Susan B. Auld
Arlington Heights, Illinois

snow flurries—
free organic carrot seeds
in today's mail

Sharon Hammer Baker
Findlay, Ohio

desire　　till the high C of spring rain

Ludmila Balabanova
Sofia, Bulgaria

toast crumbs
fall onto his paper
landslide in Peru

Mary Jo Balistreri
Waukesha, Wisconsin

Open House
the realtor nixes
the Black Lives Matter sign

Caroline Giles Banks
Minneapolis, Minnesota

a hard rain
the downspout
changes its tune

Francine Banwarth
Dubuque, Iowa

cold jail cell a jacket full of priors

Johnny Baranski
Vancouver, Washington

shoe-scraper
gap in the bristles: it fits nicely
summer beetle

Sheila K. Barksdale
Gotherington, Gloucestershire, England

chasing the wind
through a hole in the fence
a jackrabbit

Dyana Basist
Santa Cruz, California

rush hour—
"Lewis and Clark Trail"
by the interstate

Gretchen Graft Batz
Elsah, Illinois

7

my sister
catatonic now
never could reach her

Donna Bauerly
Dubuque, Iowa

peaceful
nocturnal swamp things—
crocodile's dream

MariVal Bayles
Sacramento, California

memories of a memory misplaced lilacs

Chris Bays
Beavercreek, Ohio

sea anemones—
I touch my finger to
the setting sun

Clayton Beach
Portland, Oregon

morning thunder
from the empty trough
cattle bellow

Lori Becherer
Millstadt, Illinois

charity race . . .
competing against
cherry petals

Sidney Bending
Victoria, British Columbia, Canada

river delta
a grackle spreads
its tail

Brad Bennett
Arlington, Massachusetts

the summer of love
falling into winter

Cheryl Berrong
Fairbanks, Alaska

summer solstice
tree trimmers rearrange
morning shadows

Noel Bewley
Zionsville, Indiana

the hardest part
making that leap
moss covered stone

Peggy Bilbro
Huntsville, Alabama

sea fog
the ghost story
I almost remember

Robyn Hood Black
Beaufort, South Carolina

winter wall
of winged white—
snow geese

Jim Bloss
Monroe, Washington

all around me fireflies . . .
no longer
lonely

Patsy Kate Booth
Pueblo, Colorado

Bob White
cottontail
gray fox
signatures in snow

Von S. Bourland
Happy, Texas

plum blossoms
the child slung on her hip
licks the air

Chuck Brickley
Daly City, California

visiting her
in hospice— my first step
into forever

Alan S. Bridges
Littleton, Massachusetts

brown rectangle
of dead grass and dirt
beneath the welcome mat

Chris Burdett
Loganville, Georgia

the check is in the mail . . .
only virga
this monsoon season

Alanna C. Burke
Santa Fe, New Mexico

white and black
field songs on the wing
bobolinks

Rich Burke
Phoenixville, Pennsylvania

soul searching
i punch all the buttons
in my new car

Sondra J. Byrnes
Santa Fe, New Mexico

family gathering old stories shared with the leftovers

Pris Campbell
Lake Worth, Florida

the long shadow
of a tire swing—
summer solstice

Theresa A. Cancro
Wilmington, Delaware

hum of bees
more quince blossoms
full of rain

Eleanor Carolan
Felton, California

Cycling in winter
my key finding yet again
the ice inside the lock

David Cashman
Providence, Rhode Island

egg timer
these winter bones withered
of hurry

Thomas Chockley
Plainfield, Illinois

frost rims maple leaves . . .
unseen
a woodcock dances

Paul Sleman Clark
Kensington, Maryland

the wading pool
full of fallen leaves—
the children I never had

Rick Clark
Seattle, Washington

cell phone doorbell mockingbird aria

Marcyn Del Clements
Claremont, California

bit of gossip . . .
overpruning
my roses

Lesley Clinton
Sugar Land, Texas

inauguration day
a gathering of pine needles
on the roof

Glenn G. Coats
Prospect, Virginia

moonset—
old trees laced with lichen
hover

Lysa Collins
White Rock, British Columbia, Canada

sunny it whines
raining it whines
single mosquito

Sue Colpitts
Peterborough, Ontario, Canada

the hummingbirds have gone now breakfast alone

Ellen Compton
Washington, District of Columbia

snowstorm
his statue loses
face

Jeanne Cook
South Bend, Indiana

unchanging moon
who didn't play communion
with white necco wafers

Wanda D. Cook
Hadley, Massachusetts

to capture a natural look
the camera flashes
sixty times

robyn corum
Hartselle, Alabama

parting . . .
he plucks me
a pretty weed

Amelia Cotter
Chicago, Illinois

full moon
bats inhabit
an elm's airspace

Harold Cowherd
East Lansing, Michigan

first blood pressure pill
listening for my heart
I watch as leaves unfold

Dina E Cox
Unionville, Ontario, Canada

spring showers
my resolutions
wash away

Kyle D. Craig
Indianapolis, Indiana

diploma on the wall
expectations
hanging over my head

Ronald K. Craig
Batavia, Ohio

family picnic
a thundershower
clears the air

Dan Curtis
Victoria, British Columbia, Canada

raising a toast
to distant ranges
a sip for each peak

Mark Dailey
Poultney, Vermont

family secrets
a moss-covered stonewall
in the deep woods

Carolyn Coit Dancy
Pittsford, New York

solitude
in the snowbound forest
Packer game today

Eddee Daniel
Wauwatosa, Wisconsin

Slender plant
three pointed petals
trillium

John Carl Davis
West Bend, Wisconsin

e-book
nowhere to press
a flower

Pat Davis
Pembroke, New Hampshire

night the mercy-go-round of moth wings

Cherie Hunter Day
Menlo Park, California

morning climb
among the clouds
this gnarly toe

Bill Deegan
Mahwah, New Jersey

old Japanese maple
a harsh winter
woodpecker's new home

Brian DeMuth
Bowie, Maryland

salt tinged air
a turtle's eggs deeper
into silvery sand

Angelee Deodhar
Chandigarh, India

snowed in . . .
after the piña colada
dreaming in color

Charlotte Digregorio
Winnetka, Illinois

sun-warmed sea
she takes me softly
into her mouth

Rob Dingman
Herkimer, New York

Eventually
loneliness almost becomes
anticipated

Carl Dobson
Asheville, North Carolina

consecration
the baby reaches for
a brown leaf

Kathy Donlan
Lincoln, Nebraska

change of seasons
I catch myself talking
to the wind

Margaret Dornaus
Ozark, Arkansas

a million stars
I take all night
to write one haiku

Thomas Dougherty
Baden, Pennsylvania

summer solstice
the planet and I
cross a line

Andrew O. Dugas
San Francisco, California

picking peonies
for grandmother's grave
the fields are too wet to plow

Judith Duncan
Sequim, Washington

swish of taffeta
in the courtyard
quinceañera

Lynn Edge
Tivoli, Texas

Woodworker's beech bowl—
lichen left on the edge
by design

Eric H. Edwards
Falmouth, Massachusetts

midsummer harvest—
wildflower seeds
yield butterflies

Anna Eklund-Cheong
Croissy-sur-Seine, France

song falls through
the morning silence
canyon wren

Art Elser
Denver, Colorado

So many raindrops
falling and none
in the wrong place

Bruce England
Santa Clara, California

wedding bells
the father of the bride
takes the call

Robert Epstein
El Cerrito, California

setting sail . . .
a world
without fences

Elizabeth Fanto
Timonium, Maryland

Ice cold horchata
Plantains and black beans
The peddler leaves

Alexandra G. Farolan
Vancouver, British Columbia, Canada

daffodils
the table for one
feels crowded

Ignatius Fay
Sudbury, Ontario, Canada

buttercups
at high noon
yellow2

Bruce H. Feingold
Berkeley, California

new party dress
four year old fizzes
into fairyland

Glenys Ferguson
Yass, NSW, Australia

dwarf pine . . .
figuring I've got about
ten more years

Michael Fessler
Sagamihara, Kanagawa, Japan

motionless timpani—
dragonfly cadence
of a thousand wingbeats

John Fisher
Berlin, Maryland

Raindrops
tin roof dancing
I
rocking on the porch
under polkadots of sound

Michael Fisher
Watkinsville, Georgia

first rinse of the rice
a wild scurry
of clouds

Marilyn Fleming
Pewaukee, Wisconsin

the last
of fourteen siblings
low tide

Denise Fontaine-Pincince
Belchertown, Massachusetts

white tofu
in the miso soup
winter moon

Lucia Fontana
Milan, Italy

reef sharks
guard the rusting wrecks—
my father's war

Lorin Ford
Melbourne, Victoria, Australia

Divorce proceedings
  a slight shift
    along the fault lines

Sylvia Forges-Ryan
North Haven, Connecticut

all this talk of
renunciation
the geese are flying

Mark Forrester
Hyattsville, Maryland

hungover—
asking the crow
to lower its voice

Stanford M. Forrester
Windsor, Connecticut

tending the grave
with both our names
date and dash

Robert Forsythe
Annandale, Virginia

who would have guessed
with the pulling of a tooth
the return of spring

Dale E. Foye
Bellflower, California

Gay Pride Parade
the rain recedes—
rainbow rising

Tom Lyon Freeland
Edmonton, Alberta, Canada

Passover Seder
the last of winter
in the first raindrop

Terri L. French
Huntsville, Alabama

September sun
the life guard's chair
chained to a fence

Jay Friedenberg
New York, New York

bittersweet—
the handful of blackberries
you would have brought me

Lois J. Funk
Manito, Illinois

shiny penny
in the fountain
quick change

Susan Beth Furst
Woodbridge, Virginia

melting snow
the garden Buddha
rises

Marilyn Gabel
Agawam, Massachusetts

Sierra switchbacks . . .
she loves me not,
she love me

William Scott Galasso
Laguna Woods, California

Jethro Tull ticket stubs
stuck in the back drawer,
the scent of patchouli

Cynthia Gallaher
Chicago, Illinois

forget-me-nots
past their edge the deeper blue
of the outgoing tide

Dianne Garcia
Seattle, Washington

Mount Rushmore
shadows beneath
granite eyes

Tim Gardiner
Manningtree, Essex, United Kingdom

birds in sea grass . . .
my fingers fondle
your arm hair

Marita Gargiulo
Hamden, Connecticut

game day
the peanut vender
throws a strike

Garry Gay
Windsor, California

Garage sale
memories
at a discount

Daniel J. Geltrude
Nutley, New Jersey

zen
zen
zen
there goes the dragonfly

David Gershator
St. Thomas, US Virgin Islands

OPEN ALL NIGHT
sparrow tugs a twig
behind the T

Robert Gilliland
Austin, Texas

family reunion
mockingbird's song
joins everyone's chatter

Joette Giorgis
Port St. Lucie, Florida

night clouds
   signing   our
          divorce

Scott Glander
Glenview, Illinois

finding her way
to a shelter
wood violets

Susan Godwin
Madison, Wisconsin

unknown bird
known to others
with better books

Kevin Goldstein-Jackson
Dorset, England

lilac scent—
how long must i go on
remembering

John Gonzalez
Ipswich, Suffolk, England

somewhere dark
my old Dumbo
in the dump

Harry Goodheart
Tryon, North Carolina

going with the f
                low tide anemone

LeRoy Gorman
Napanee, Ontario, Canada

her suicide
snow devils twist
across the field

joan iversen goswell
Valencia, Pennsylvania

one sneeze
and then two
a bowl full of daisies

June Gray
Great Falls, Montana

zigzagging
down the straight path
poison ivy

Steve Greene
Haddon Township, New Jersey

the usual
boy leaves girl story
assisted living

Anita Guenin
San Diego, California

walking in the woods
I find that I too am stirred
by the wind's quiet

Lucia Kiersch Haase
Spring Valley, Illinois

sitting zazen
on inauguration day
the rain

Johnnie Johnson Hafernik
San Francisco, California

family home
almost bare—
her gold thimble

Maureen Lanagan Haggerty
Madison, New Jersey

spring café
grandma takes out
her red lipstick

John J. Han
Manchester, Missouri

refrigerator magnets
all the places
her friends have been

Patty Hardin
Long Beach, Washington

PDA
virtually
inseparable

C.R. Harper
Snohomish, Washington

snowbound
the highway drifts off the road
and into the trees

Devin Harrison
Duncan, British Columbia, Canada

predawn quake
the ungodly clamor
of our trinkets

William Hart
Montrose, California

forgiven . . .
rills of snowmelt
seek the river

Michele L. Harvey
Hamilton, New York

wheelchair stroll
the snap crackle pop
of autumn leaves

Patricia Harvey
East Lonmeadow, Massachusetts

into that silence
that void of just ceased rain
a slight breeze lifts me

Arch Haslett
Toronto, Ontario, Canada

who cares
if no one believes me?
triple rainbow

John Hawk
Columbus, Ohio

shopping
for perennials—
new wedding rings

Tia Haynes
Cuyahoga Falls, Ohio

first transfusion
the potted geraniums
a brighter red

Merle Hinchee
Houma, Louisiana

scenic overlook
the mallard's nest hidden
by wild grass

Carolyn M. Hinderliter
Phoenix, Arizona

New Year
first kiss
from an old flame

Judith Hishikawa
West Burke, Vermont

autumn afternoon not just leaves that fall a funeral
procession

Mark Hitri
Fort Worth, Texas

old pond
her clothes
not folded

Jeff Hoagland
Hopewell, New Jersey

listening . . .
to the sound of summer's marching
flip-flop flip-flop flip-flop

Jean Holland
Albany, New York

at the gull's feet—
the ocean spreads itself
thin

Gary Hotham
Scaggsville, Maryland

jumping in the dumpster
with his lifelong mate—
winter raven

Ruth Holzer
Herndon, Virginia

puffy spring clouds
　　a spill
　　　of paper
　　　　cutouts

Elizabeth Howard
Arlington, Tennessee

sagebrush flats
　　　mirror the low clouds
sharps of birdsong

Marshall Hryciuk
Toronto, Ontario, Canada

squeezing beneath the eaves
the accordionist
still rained upon

David Jacobs
London, United Kingdom

far offshore
a fish leaps
no sound

Eric Jennings
Atlanta, Georgia

"There is metastasis"
the prairie field
mow or let bloom?

Kathy Johnson
Waukesha, Wisconsin

knot pine floors
furballs pirouette
behind the corn broom

Tami M. Johnson
Birmingham, Alabama

garden cleanup
a rusty, full moon rises
beyond factory haze

Jean Jorgensen
Edmonton, Alberta

another day in paradise lost in translation

Jim Kacian
Winchester, Virginia

early spring
answering to no one
north wind

Barbara Kaufmann
Massapequa Park, New York

beneath the pines
decomposing layers
of music

Julie Bloss Kelsey
Germantown, Maryland

spring cleaning
on the tow truck's long flatbed
another tow truck

Phillip Kennedy
Monterey, California

old western
the sheriff walks thru
a black and white world

Michael Ketchek
Rochester, New York

Lee Square
a crane came by night
to remove a statue

Howard Lee Kilby
Hot Springs National Park, Arkansas

ghost town . . .
the cowboy clicks
his heels three times

Maureen Kingston
Wayne, Nebraska

night trawler
he catches the moon
in his net

Mary Kipps
Sterling, Virginia

church bells
on Saturday—
uneven flagstones

kjmunro
Whitehorse, Yukon Territory, Canada

evening—
still hearing the sirens
from this morning

Samantha Klein
Baton Rouge, Louisiana

morning fog
a carpenter calls
for a 2 x 4

Joann Klontz
Fulton, Maryland

hovering leaf—
old wishes
do they sink or rise up?

Marylouise Knight
Omaha, Nebraska

thunder sky
on the horizon
their argument

Dianne Koch
Dubuque, Iowa

Earth Day
getting heavy
all these people

Deb Koen
Rochester, New York

not what you seem
under the surface
water on Mars

Deborah P Kolodji
Temple City, California

Match Play
First Round
All Square

Ed Kosiewicz
Punta Gorda, Florida

despite the chill   trillium

S.M. Kozubek
Sarasota, Florida

at the ice cream parlor
girls with pistachio & black raspberry
toenails

Henry W. Kreuter
Lebanon, New Jersey

koi tickle lilies
in blissful serenity
summer symmetry

Alexis Krysyna
Pacific Grove, California

February rain
a string of pearls
on bare branches

Ron LaMarsh
Seattle, Washington

scarecrow
never more
the family farm

Jill Lange
Cleveland Heights, Ohio

another typo
in my book
no one has read

David G. Lanoue
New Orleans, Louisiana

I haven't
been drinking
hazy moon

Jim Laurila
Florence, Massachusetts

glittering path
down the width of a river
rolls the moon

Michael Henry Lee
St. Augustine, Florida

insomnia the length of four trains

Phyllis Lee
Sebring, Ohio

Father's Day
I cook bacon and eggs
again without you

Brenda Lempp
Madison, Wisconsin

winter solstice
the night train whistle
colors the cold

Antoinette Libro
St. Augustine, Florida

our argument
I test some rocks to cross
the river

Cyndi Lloyd
Riverton, Utah

in paint box colors
oak and maple leaves
free fall

Renee Londner
Prospect, Connecticut

equinox
the weight
of dying light

Gregory Longenecker
Pasadena, California

sun clock . . .
my day unwinds
with low-flying sparrows

Amy Losak
Teaneck, New Jersey

raking leaves
the wind and I
take turns

Bob Lucky
Jubail, Eastern Province, Saudi Arabia

cherry blossom petals
fall into the gutter—
spring rain . . .

E. Luke
Palos Verdes Peninsula, California

cherry blossom tour—
17 shades of pink
to please everyone

Janis Albright Lukstein
Palos Verdes Peninsula, California

sizzle of rain on the cold lake acupuncture

Doris Lynch
Bloomington, Indiana

winter tide
scattering his ashes
on the rocks

Jone Rush MacCulloch
Portland, Oregon

lost among aspen and pine
it wanders through the canyon—
autumn wind

Patricia J. Machmiller
San Jose, California

winter solitaire—
again and again
I draw the joker

Carole MacRury
Point Roberts, Washington

faint stars
she puts her daughter to bed
in the back seat

Ann Magyar
Boston, Massachusetts

midsummer
the glide
between breast strokes

Hannah Mahoney
Cambridge, Massachusetts

tendrils of fog
I follow a thread
back into the dream

Annette Makino
Arcata, California

soaring gulls—
four soldiers
lower the coffin

Ruth Marcus
Sequim, Washington

the Milky Way—
tell me
about deep water

Jeannie Martin
Arlington, Massachusetts

cloud after cloud
the many-windowed prison
at Sing Sing

Michael McClintock
Clovis, California

migrating monarch
alighting on a milkweed pod
open border

Wilma McCracken
Downers Grove, Illinois

distant forest fire
the tanager
we only hear

Tanya McDonald
Woodinville, Washington

lines in sand
    lines on my face
years of shoreline

Marci McGill
Cincinnati, Ohio

behind barbed wire
the free play
of dandelions

Marietta Jane McGregor
Canberra, Australian Capital Territory, Australia

memorial bench
the shadow of a crow
passes by

Leanne McIntosh
Nanaimo, British Columbia, Canada

cornfield maze
the tightening circles
of a red-tailed hawk

Joe McKeon
Strongsville, Ohio

ninety-six last week
renewing her subscription
she checks three years

Dorothy McLaughlin
Somerset, New Jersey

morning run
a great blue heron folds itself
into the sky

Elizabeth McMunn-Tetangco
Merced, California

gardening . . .
the cat too
sprays the flowers

Robert B McNeill
Winchester, Virginia

hummingbird
where the feeder
was

Peter Meister
Huntsville, Alabama

the cowhand lifts
the branding iron from the coals—
summer sunrise

Sarah E. Metzler
Marion Center, Pennsylvania

all night love
the candle
reshapes itself

Jayne Miller
Hazel Green, Wisconsin

shifting embers
the glow of everyone
breathing

Ben Moeller-Gaa
St. Louis, Missouri

thin ice
the crackling sound
when she breathes

Beverly Acuff Momoi
Mountain View, California

juxtaposition
my mind
elsewhere

Mike Montreuil
Ottawa, Ontario, Canada

lamppost shadow
on the broken sidewalk
evening sun

Lenard D. Moore
Raleigh, North Carolina

opal moon
the scarecrow with
bottle cap eyes

Ron C. Moss
Leslie Vale, Tasmania, Australia

night-blooming basswoods
how easy it should be
to fall in love

Marsh Muirhead
Bemidji, Minnesota

the fragrance
of sub-alpine firs
Hurricane Ridge

Leanne Mumford
Sydney, New South Wales, Australia

lilac grows wild—
you will not be forgotten
gravestone epitaph

Sandra J Nantais
Ruston, Louisiana

dive-
bombed
by
a
rain
drop
another
moment
older

Peter Newton
Winchendon, Massachusetts

a memoir
from the lizard shedding its tail
still wriggling

Suzanne Niedzielska
Glastonbury, Connecticut

layer of snow
the daffodils
bend lower

Patti Niehoff
Cincinnati, Ohio

evensong
across the meadow
her ashes sing

Nika
Victoria, British Columbia, Canada

spring dreams
hang from a waning arc
snow moon

Patricia Nolan
Colorado Springs, Colorado

spring break
a mallard drake and hen
at the travel agent's door

Catherine Anne Nowaski
Rochester, New York

Southern "Nutcracker"
backstage, again and again
whispered "'scuse me."

David Oates
Athens, Georgia

An awakening
Dreams of fire and brimstone
Slowly fade away

Elizabeth Obih-Frank
Irvington, New York

a collared dove
lands on a weathercock
faint thunder

Polona Oblak
Ljubljana, Slovenia

a quiver of ships
lined up facing toward port
pregnant with cargo

Frank O'Brien
West Bloomfield, Michigan

drunken stupor
2 + 2 equals
a debate

Karen O'Leary
West Fargo, North Dakota

country roads
reflections of light
from new steel roofs

Ellen Grace Olinger
Oostburg, Wisconsin

a sea turtle
inked on her shoulder,
off-shore breeze

Bob Oliveira
Bonita Springs, Florida

canopy of cattails
a wispy sight of
butterfly wings

Frances O'Neill
Coon Rapids, Minnesota

the theology of barnacles my thoughts becoming

Renée Owen
Sebastopol, California

A_m I

Roland Packer
Hamilton, Ontario, Canada

campfire
the storyteller's shadow
reaches the woods

Tom Painting
Atlanta, Georgia

gathering storm
the crowd passes petitions
to new arrivals

Kathe L. Palka
Flemington, New Jersey

waiting to catch
my wandering mind—
dusty Buddha

Sarah Paris
San Francisco, California

parkway traffic slow enough for crickets

James A. Paulson
Narberth, Pennsylvania

migrant workers
digging potatoes . . .
the hollow hearts

Bill Pauly
Asbury, Iowa

snow melt
briefly my dog's tracks
wolf-size

Jacquie Pearce
Vancouver, British Columbia, Canada

moving day
treasures wrapped in bubble
memories wrapped in air

Patricia Pella
Bristol, Rhode Island

late-April moon
just a thin smile
after taxes

Ann M Penton
Green Valley, Arizona

pinned to the wall winter sunshine

Gregory Piko
Yass, New South Wales, Australia

speck of a plane
soon the clouds
cover the hum

Madhuri Pillai
Melbourne, Australia

new guitar
I strum a few chords
in the mirror

Robert Piotrowski
Mississauga, Ontario, Canada

woodland water over stones beer cans

Marian M. Poe
Plano, Texas

Zen garden
emptiness
in full bloom

Marilyn Powell
Morristown, New Jersey

final exam
the probability
of becoming dust

Joan Prefontaine
Cottonwood, Arizona

monarch migration
it begins again
my life story

Sharon Pretti
San Francisco, California

birthday wishes
a brand new box
of pills

Vanessa Proctor
Sydney, New South Wales, Australia

summer heat
a bullfrog belly-flops
into the pond

John Quinnett
Bryson City, North Carolina

full moon morning
even the crows
look up in silence

David Rachlin
Stow, Massachusetts

hanging heavy
icicles from roof edge
my winter mood

Barth H. Ragatz
Fort Wayne, Indiana

thrush's nest
somewhere in those eggs . . .
the melody

Katherine Raine
Milton, Otago, New Zealand

benediction
the temptation to
check my phone

Holli Rainwater
Fresno, Ohio

my sister and I
step on each other's shadow
last slant of daylight

Nancy Rapp
St. Louis, Missouri

squash blossoms
in the garden that was
hers— and butterflies

Melanie A. Rawls
Tallahasse, Florida

synching
with the rainbow
I arch my back

Ann Rawson
Glasgow, Scotland

the stone Buddha's toenails
large enough
to sit on

Dian Duchin Reed
Soquel, California

winter thunder . . .
waiting for the buffalo
at Standing Rock

Joanne M. Reinbold
Wilmington, Delaware

Jazz apples for sale
hand picked Trademark

David H. Rembert, Jr.
Columbia, South Carolina

three strands of ivy
encircle the smooth bark . . .
her tattoo

Sue Richards
Birmingham, England

late to bed—
the pillow you use
to divide us

Bryan Rickert
Belleville, Illinois

red sunset
the flame of her hair
lighting me

Edward J. Rielly
Westbrook, Maine

at the rim of Vesuvius . . .
cigarette smoke

Julie Riggott
Glendale, California

restringing fence wire—
the meadowlark's song one post
ahead of the wind

Chad Lee Robinson
Pierre, South Dakota

touching tank
the anemone gets a feel
for the real me

Michele Root-Bernstein
East Lansing, Michigan

In the parking lot
he held the Mumms
like a baby

David H. Rosen
Eugene, Oregon

deep cold night
under the bright stars
a perfect world

Bruce Ross
Hampden, Maine

Telling
its story
gurgle of the creek

Alexis Rotella
Arnold, Maryland

assisted living
an unmatched sock
in the dryer

Raymond Roy
Winston-Salem, North Carolina

door   open
gate   ajar
dog gone
doggone

Maggie Roycraft
Morristown, New Jersey

winter moon
in deep craters
insomnia

Lidia Rozmus
Vernon Hills, Illinois

rainy afternoon
slug on a mum

Patricia McKernon Runkle
Short Hills, New Jersey

rickety barn
she breeds dogs
on a budget

Margaret Rutley
Victoria, British Columbia, Canada

her skin not a petal yet in bloom

Tom Sacramona
Plainville, Massachusetts

formal bows and gowns
of ancient Chinese lovers
leaves drift in slow waves

Clarise Samuels
Montreal, Quebec, Canada

this bamboo
stretching hollowness
as it grows

Srinivasa Rao Sambangi
Hyderabad, Telangana, India

billowing clouds
followed by claims of fake news
we chew on the words

Judith Morrison Schallberger
San Jose, California

chlorinated pool
a frog leaps in
and croaks

Mike Schoenburg
Skokie, Illinois

empty cocoon
you say you believe
in life after death

Olivier Schopfer
Geneva, Switzerland

no shore
that does not touch us
gravitational waves

Ann K. Schwader
Westminster, Colorado

dirt for the grave
going back
just as it is

Dan Schwerin
Greendale, Wisconsin

beads of rain
last year's christmas
ornaments

Patrick Shannon
Calgary, Alberta, Canada

fork in the trail...
a yellow butterfly
leads to the right

Adelaide B. Shaw
Millbrook, New York

dancing outside
through heavy rain . . .
memories pouring

Kendra E. Shaw
San Diego, California

unshelled pistachios
my father
on marriage

Tiffany Shaw-Diaz
Dayton, Ohio

transcontinental—
settling into the sway
of the coach

Michael Sheffield
Kenwood, California

distant motorcycle
cool wind rushing
through the willow

Nancy Shires
Greenville, North Carolina

canned hunt
big men surround
the buffet

Gary Simpson
Fairview Heights, Illinois

afternoon thunder
the copier
jammed again

Karen Sites
Boulder, Colorado

the crossword puzzle
same words, different meanings
mother and daughter

Amy Skinner
Pine Mountain, Georgia

rainy afternoon . . .
one of many puddles
holds a golden leaf

D.W. Skrivseth
St. Anthony, Minnesota

July in Minnesota
trading fireworks
for fireflies

Carole Slesnick
Bellingham, Washington

tambourine . . .
the toothless busker's dog
drops the hat

Michael Smeer
Hoofddorp, The Netherlands

100th birthday—
a balloon caught
in the powerline

Crystal Simone Smith
Durham, North Carolina

earth day concludes
horizon's dull glow
one star in view

K.O. Smith
Asheville, North Carolina

autumn wind
the old screen door
fits

Steven Smolak
Murphysboro, Illinois

the loose-plank grumble
of a country bridge
cumulonimbus

Barbara Snow
Eugene, Oregon

fallen leaves
the baby bump
gets smaller

Nicholas M. Sola
New Orleans, Louisiana

wishing I knew
their language
night-calling migrants

Sheila Sondik
Bellingham, Washington

he said, she said
the Many Worlds
interpretation

Robert Sorrels
Brazil, Indiana

pre-storm stillness
the colour of the sky
an old bruise

susan spooner
Victoria, British Columbia, Canada

seaside town
I long to walk
on clouds again

Carmen Sterba
University Place, Washington

Father's Day fishing . . .
his lure
still dances

Jeff Stillman
Norwich, New York

coffee house jazz
the barista blends
his rendition of chai

Michael Stinson
Omaha, Nebraska

birthday cake at 90
her reluctance
to blow the candles out

Stevie Strang
Laguna Niguel, California

the whistle
of a wood duck . . .
her last breath

Debbie Strange
Winnipeg, Manitoba, Canada

winter moonlight—
the rise and fall of her
remaining breast

Lee Strong
Rochester, New York

antique shop....
post card message
still job hunting

William C. Stuart
Clinton, Connecticut

sun bleached driftwood—
kids back to school next week

Jim Sullivan
Glenview, Illinois

dusk—
one last leaf anchors
the spider web

Dean Summers
Seattle, Washington

oshiguma
the dog returns
my scowl

Sneha Sundaram
Jersey City, New Jersey

summer snow
groom's cold feet

Suzanne Vacany Surles
Jacksonville, North Carolina

this restlessness . . .
compost piles
in five or six states

Lesley Anne Swanson
Coopersburg, Pennsylvania

abandoned church
barred windows reflect
autumn moon

Polly W. Swafford
Kansas City, Missouri

oxytocin vs. cortisol
the view from the tip
of the hoodoo

George Swede
Toronto, Ontario, Canada

sunset walk
a pool of gold
at the rainbow's end

Barbara Tate
Winchester, Tennessee

man-made lake
swimming in
our own imaginations

Dietmar Tauchner
Puchberg, Austria

camera obscura
the upside-down
of laughter

Angela Terry
Lake Forest Park, Washington

insomnia
sheep missing
from the count

Jennifer Thiermann
Glenview, Illinois

now the wild geese
now the far-off child
call and call

Richard Tice
Kent, Washington

Veterans Day tai chi—
distant strains of
the Shores of Tripoli

Deanna Tiefenthal
Rochester, New York

Julia Child's cracked spine;
she always falls open
at boeuf bourguignon

Charles Trumbull
Santa Fe, New Mexico

the chop, chop of Hueys
our war returns
in color

Del Todey Turner
Waterloo, Iowa

Lotuses laugh
Bathing in the moonlight
All color bleached

VeerajaR
Franklin, Tennessee

No lovely gesture
When my dog licks at my face
It's simply the salt

Barry Vitcov
Ashland, Oregon

spring morning
dust bunnies faster
than the mop

Marilyn Appl Walker
Madison, Georgia

first snow
the coyote
on our welcome mat

Diane Wallihan
Port Townsend, Washington

God counting out his stars
flicks one across the sky
just for me

Mary Zan Warren
Fritch, Texas

rainless . . .
the brush
of a lacewing

Julie Warther
Dover, Ohio

recounting her vertebrae—
the midnight silence
of never

Lew Watts
Santa Fe, New Mexico

swallows' nest
curling down its edges
white seagull feathers

Mary Weidensaul
Granby, Massachusetts

stone wall in sunshine
eighteen skinks
some in pairs

Linda Weir
Bowie, Maryland

ate for the bus—
petals swirl
in a hearse's wake

Michael Dylan Welch
Sammamish, Washington

loud debate
or indiscreet gossip
hot air balloon lift-off

Christine Wenk-Harrison
Lago Vista, Texas

twittering
goldfinches actually
brief and to the point

Sharon R. Wesoky
Meadville, Pennsylvania

hoarfrost
veiling the trees
our silent drive

Daniel White
Beaumont, California

dancing
with my shadow
a cloudless sulphur

Robin White
Deerfield, New Hampshire

after a heart stent
I, too, need to be pruned
withered garden

Neal Whitman
Pacific Grove, California

thin ice on the pond
how close I am
to breaking

Scott Wiggerman
Albuquerque, New Mexico

autumn rain
I'll die knowing all the words
to so many songs

Billie Wilson
Juneau, Alaska

peephole
on the ferry floor
the wild bay at bay

Kath Abela Wilson
Pasadena, California

an old birdhouse
where the fire is blue
smoke rising into empty sky

Robert Witmer
Tokyo, Japan

sway of the candle flame
the wake
of your words

Valorie Broadhurst Woerdehoff
Dubuque, Iowa

heat lightning
the conductor swells
the string section

Alison Woolpert
Santa Cruz, California

a butterfly lands
I walk with you
guiding your tiny steps

Sharon Yee
Torrance, California

budding leaves
the mockingbird queues up
a new song

Karina M. Young
Salinas, California

summer's end
the last bar
of ice cream

Lori Zajkowski
New York, New York

frangipani lei
the hula line dance
of bees

J. Zimmerman
Santa Cruz, California

Acknowledgements

The editor wishes to express gratitude to Mike Montreuil for the opportunity to edit this year's anthology, Dianne Garcia for assistance with membership queries, Luminita Suse for the cover and, of course, members for submitting their best writing.

Publication Credits

Fred Andrle— *hedgerow*, 99, December, 2016

Bett Angel-Stawarz— *Windfall Australian Haiku*, 3, 2015

frances angela— *Lilliput Review*, 197, Autumn 2016

Fay Aoyagi— *Mariposa*, 37, Spring/Summer 2017

Marilyn Ashbaugh— *Modern Haiku*, 48:1, 2017

Susan B. Auld— *Modern Haiku*, 48:1, Winter Spring, 2017

Ludmila Balabanova— *Modern Haiku*, 47.1, Winter-Spring, 2016

Mary Jo Balistreri— *Failed Haiku*, 20, November, 2016

Francine Banwarth— *The Heron's Nest*, 18, 2016

Johnny Baranski— *Otata*, 12, December 2016

Dyana Basist— *Geppo*, 42:2, 2017

MariVal Bayles— *Gypsy's Haiku*, Createspace, 2016

Chris Bays— *Bones*, 12, March 2017

Clayton Beach— *Wild Plum*, Fall/Winter 2016

Lori Becherer— *Chrysanthemum*, 20, October 2016

Sidney Bending— Honourable Mention, *2014 Vancouver Cherry Blossom Festival Haiku Invitational*

Von S. Bourland— *Austin Poetry Society Anthology*, 2009

Sondra J. Byrnes— *DailyHaiku*, Cycle 20, Winter 2015

Theresa A. Cancro— *Modern Haiku*, 47:3, Fall 2016

Lesley Clinton— *Frogpond*, 38:3, 2015

Ellen Compton— *Presence*, 54, 2016

Jeanne Cook— *Geppo*, 33:6, 2009

Wanda D. Cook— *bottle rockets*, 33, 2015

robyn corum— *bottle rockets*, 34, June 2016

Amelia Cotter— *Modern Haiku*, 45:2, Summer 2014

Carolyn Coit Dancy— *The Heron's Nest*, Vol. XVII No. 4, 2015

Pat Davis— *Failed Haiku: Journal of English Senryu*, October 2016

Cherie Hunter Day— *moongarlic*, 8, May 2017

Bill Deegan— *Frogpond*, 35: 2, 2012

Charlotte Digregorio— *The Heron's Nest*, Vol. XVII, No. 2, June 2015

Margaret Dornaus— *Prayer for the Dead*, Singing Moon Press, 2016

Thomas Dougherty— *Frogpond*, 37:1, Winter 2014

Andrew O. Dugas— *Wild Plum*, 1:2, Fall & Winter 2015

Lynn Edge— *Lifting the Sky*, Dos Gatos Press, 2013

Glenys Ferguson— Amelia Fielden and Noriko Tanaka, *Poems to Wear: From Japan and Australia*, 2016

Lucia Fontana— *Charlotte Digregorio's Writer's Blog*, January 10th, 2017

Lorin Ford— *Frogpond*, 39:1, Winter, 2016

Sylvia Forges-Ryan— *What Light There Is*, Red Moon Press, 2016

Mark Forrester— *Lilliput Review*, 195, 2015

Lois J. Funk— *Mayfly*, 60, Winter 2016

Susan Beth Furst— *Blithe Spirit*, 27:1, February 2017

LeRoy Gorman— *The Heron's Nest*, June 2017

joan iversen goswell— *Modern Haiku*, 48:1, Winter-Spring 2017

Anita Guenin— 2nd Place (senryu), The San Francisco International Competition for Haiku, Senryu & Tanka, 2016

Patty Hardin— *Frogpond*, 38:3, 2015

Devin Harrison— *Presence*, 56, 2016

William Hart— *On Cat Time*, Timberline Press, 2004

Patricia Harvey— *New England Letters*, 58, 2016

John Hawk— *hedgerow*, 110, Spring 2017

Gary Hotham— *South by Southeast*, 3:4, 1996

Tami M. Johnson— *The Heron's Nest,* 16: 1, March 2014

Jim Kacian— *NOON*, 10, 2014

Barbara Kaufmann— *Failed Haiku*, 2:15, March 2017

Julie Bloss Kelsey— *Rattle*, 49, Fall 2015

Joann Klontz— *The Heron's Nest*, 6, 2004

Deb Koen— *Haiku Canada Review*, 10:2, October 2016

Deborah P Kolodji— *Star*Line*, 40.1, Winter 2017

S.M. Kozubek— *is/let*, November, 2016

Jill Lange— *Failed Haiku*, March 2016

Gregory Longenecker— First Place, Irish Haiku Society 2016 Haiku/Senryu Contest

Amy Losak— *Asahi Haikuist Network*, Aug. 5, 2016; *Daily Haiku*, Aug. 14, 2016

Bob Lucky— *Presence*, 48, Spring 2013

E. Luke— *Geppo*, May 2017

Janis Albright Lukstein— *Geppo*, May 2017

Patricia J. Machmiller— *tinywords*, 16:2, 2016

Annette Makino— *Frogpond*, 40:1, Winter 2017

Jeannie Martin— *a circle of breath*, baby buddha press, 2016

Tanya McDonald— *Mariposa*, 34, Spring-Summer 2016

Marietta Jane McGregor— *bottle rockets*, 36, February 2017

Elizabeth McMunn-Tetangco— *Akitsu Quarterly*, Spring 2017

Robert B. McNeill— *Moonset*, 5:1, Spring/Summer 2009

Sarah E. Metzler— *Modern Haiku*, 48:2, Summer 2017

Jayne Miller— *Acorn*, 27, 2012

Ben Moeller-Gaa— *The Heron's Nest*, 19:1, 2017

Mike Montreuil— *Haiku Canada Review*, 10:1, February 2016

Lenard D. Moore— *Right Hand Pointing*, 95, Winter Haiku 2016

Ron C. Moss— *Modern Haiku*, 47:1, 2016

Marsh Muirhead— *Acorn*, 29, Fall 2012

Peter Newton— *Modern Haiku*, 47:2, Spring 2016

Karen O'Leary— *Sonic Boom*, 7, December 2016

Ellen Grace Olinger— *EarthRise Rolling Haiku Collaboration 2015: The Year of Light*, The Haiku Foundation

Renée Owen— *Modern Haiku*, 48:1, Winter-Spring 2017

Roland Packer— *Modern Haiku,* 46:1, Spring 2015

Tom Painting— *Modern Haiku*, 47:2, Spring 2016

Bill Pauly— *Frogpond*, 12:2, Spring/Summer 1989

Ann M Penton— *Wisconsin Poets' Calendar*, 2010

Gregory Piko— *Between Waves*, Red Moon Press, 2015

Chad Lee Robinson— *Mariposa*, 35, Fall/Winter 2016

Tom Sacramona— *moongarlic*, 7, November 2016

Olivier Schopfer— *Failed Haiku, A Journal of English Senryu,* 1:11, November 2016

Ann K. Schwader— *Star*Line,* 39: 4, Fall 2016

Tiffany Shaw-Diaz— *Frogpond,* 40:1, Winter 2017

D. W. Skrivseth— Robert Epstein, *The Sacred in Contemporary Haiku,* 2017

Crystal Simone Smith— *Frogpond,* 39.2, Spring/ Summer 2016

Sheila Sondik— *tinywords,*15.1, March 2015

Jeff Stillman— *Acorn,* #38, Spring 2017

Debbie Strange— Honorable Mention, *Betty Drevniok Award,* 2015

Lee Strong— *Modern Haiku,* 45:2, Summer 2014

George Swede— *Haiku Canada Review,* 11:1, February 2017

Barbara Tate— *NeverEnding Story,* June, 2016

Dietmar Tauchner— *NOON,* 13, March 2017

Richard Tice— *OUTCH,* 4:2-3, 1979

Marilyn Walker— *Modern Haiku,* 43:1, 2012

Lew Watts— *Frogpond,* 39.2, Spring/Summer 2016

Scott Wiggerman— *cattails,* April 2017

Kath Abela Wilson— *Akitsu,* Spring, 2017

Valorie Broadhurst Woerdehoff— *Failed Haiku,* 1:7, July 2016

Sharon Yee— *What the Wind Can't Touch,* Southern California Haiku Study Group Anthology, 2016

Index of Poets

133